bake me I'm yours...
Christmas

D&C

David and Charles

www.bakeme.com

A DAVID & CHARLES BOOK
© F&W Media International, LTD 2011

David & Charles is an imprint of F&W Media
International, LTD
Brunel House, Forde Close, Newton Abbot,
TQ12 4PU, UK

F&W Media International, LTD is a subsidiary
of F+W Media Inc.
4700 East Galbraith Road, Cincinnati,
OH 45236, USA

First published in the UK and USA in 2011

Text and designs © Lindy Smith, Zoe Clark,
Maisie Parrish, Joan & Graham Belgrove,
Tracey Mann 2011
Layout and photography © F&W Media
International, LTD 2011

Lindy Smith, Zoe Clark, Maisie Parrish, Joan
& Graham Belgrove and Tracey Mann have
asserted their rights to be identified as authors
of this work in accordance with the Copyright,
Designs and Patents Act, 1988.

The authors and publisher have made every
effort to ensure that all the instructions in the
book are accurate and safe, and therefore
cannot accept liability for any resulting injury,
damage or loss to persons or property,
however it may arise.

Names of manufacturers and other products are
provided for the information of readers, with no
intention to infringe copyright or trademarks.

A catalogue record for this book is available
from the British Library.

ISBN-13: 978-1-4463-0060-2 hardback
ISBN-10: 1-4463-0060-9 hardback

Printed in China by RR Donnelley
for F&W Media International, LTD
Brunel House, Forde Close, Newton Abbot,
TQ12 4PU, UK

10 9 8 7 6 5 4 3 2 1

Publisher Alison Myer
Desk Editor Jeni Hennah
Project Editor Alison Smith
Senior Designers Jodie Lystor and Victoria Marks
Photographers Lorna Yabsley, Sian Irvine, Kim
Sayer, Simon Whitmore and Karl Adamson
Production Manager Bev Richardson

F+W Media Inc. publishes high-quality books
on a wide range of subjects. For more great
book ideas visit: **www.rucraft.co.uk**

Contents

introduction

Whether you're looking for quick treats for guests, delicious desserts for Christmas dinner or cute edible decorations for your tree, there's something to suit every taste. These tempting projects are sure to delight friends and family during the festive season.

Festive Favourites shows you how to create impressive cakes to feed the whole family. **Tasty Treats** explores an array of scrumptious cakes and cookies, which make perfect party food. **Delicious Decorations** showcases a range of creations that will make fabulous trimmings for your table or tree. Finally, **Perfect Presents** features a range of edible gifts that will delight all who receive them!

There are various festive recipes to treat yourself and your family, from traditional fruit cake and spicy gingerbread to indulgent chocolate brownies and wonderfully rich truffles. The techniques section includes everything you need to know to bake and decorate your creations with different icings, pastes and embellishments.

The possibilities are endless, so be inspired to design your own wonderful cakes, cupcakes, cookies and chocolates. What are you waiting for – go on and enjoy creating your Christmas bakes!

tools and equipment

Before you begin to bake you will need to ensure that you have the right equipment to hand. It is worth familiarizing yourself with them and getting to grips with the basic recipes and techniques first, so that you can easily achieve results to impress your friends and family.

baking equipment

* baking trays and tins
* cooling racks
* cupcake cases
* cutters
* food mixer or hand-held mixer
* food processor or hand-held whisk
* greaseproof paper
* measuring spoons and jug
* mixing bowl
* rolling pin
* sieve
* spatula
* kitchen scales

Food mixing can be done by hand if you don't have an electric mixer

decorating equipment

* **chocolate moulds** – for tempered chocolate
* **craft knife** – for intricate cutting tasks
* **cutters** – for embossing and cutting paste
* **paintbrushes** – a range of sizes used for stippling, painting and dusting
* **paint palette** – for mixing paste colours and dusts prior to painting
* **palette knife** – for cutting paste and spreading buttercream
* **piping tubes (tips)** – for piping royal icing and cutting out small circles
* **disposable piping (pastry) bags**
* **rolling pin** – non-stick and textured
* **scissors** – for cutting transfer sheets to size
* **spacers** – to achieve an even thickness when rolling out paste
* **non-stick board** – for rolling out pastes
* **Dresden tool** – for creating marks on paste
* **cutting wheel** – used instead of a knife to avoid dragging the paste
* **quilting tool** – used to add stitching lines to paste
* **smoother** – to create a smooth, even finish when covering cakes with paste
* **sugar shaper and disc** – for shaping paste

Festive Favourites

chocolate wreath

This rich chocolate cake makes a decadent alternative to a traditional fruit cake. Decorated with chocolate holly leaves, berries, cinnamon sticks and Christmas roses, it is sure to bring out the festive spirit in everyone! The gold organza ribbon and red holly berries add extra sparkle to this sumptuous festive treat. You can adapt the wreath design or make a simpler version just using holly leaves.

Beautiful roses made from white chocolate paste are combined with dark chocolate holly leaves and cigarillos to create a stylish, contemporary wreath.

you will need ...

* 20cm (8in) round chocolate cake
* 28cm (11in) round cake board
* 1kg (2lb 4oz) milk chocolate paste
* 250g (9oz) dark chocolate paste
* 100g (3½oz) white chocolate paste
* 25g (1oz) dark couverture chocolate
* chocolate buttercream
* 9 dark chocolate cigarillos
* Dresden tool
* flower cutter
* holly cutter
* bright gold and frosted flame dusting powder
* sugar shaper
* disposable piping (pastry) bag and piping tube (tip)
* gold ribbon: 4cm (1½in), 1.5cm (⅝in) and 3mm (⅛in) wide

1 Prepare the 20cm (8in) round chocolate cake and place onto the 28cm (11in) round board. Spread a thick layer of buttercream over the cake and cover with milk chocolate paste.

2 Roll out a long strip of milk chocolate paste, paint a little cooled boiled water onto the cake board and attach the paste. Use a textured rolling pin to make a pattern around the edge and cut off any excess paste with a palette knife.

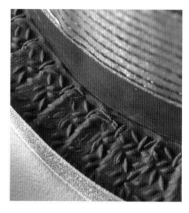

3 Roll out 200g (7oz) of dark chocolate paste onto some icing sugar and use a medium metal holly cutter to cut out 35 holly leaves. Mark the veins of the holly with a Dresden tool and leave to dry for about 10 minutes.

4 Roll out 100g (3½oz) of white chocolate paste and use the flower cutter to cut out 5 white flowers. Frill the edges of each flower using a textured rolling pin and leave to dry for approximately 10 minutes.

5 Load the sugar shaper with a small amount of white chocolate paste. Squeeze the shaper then remove a little paste with a Dresden tool and place into the centre of each flower. Dust the centre with some bright gold dusting powder.

6 Gently heat a sharp knife with some dry heat and use to carefully cut the cigarillos in half. Arrange three cigarillos together and tie with the 3mm (⅛in) gold ribbon.

7 Roll some dark chocolate paste into small balls for the holly berries and dust with frosted flame dusting powder.

8 Temper 25g (1oz) of dark couverture chocolate, place in a disposable piping (pastry) bag and use to attach the holly, berries, Christmas roses and cigarillos in a wreath formation.

9 Tie the 4cm (1½in) ribbon around the cake and finish with a bow. Attach the 1.5cm (⅝in) ribbon to the edge of the cake board.

The chocolate decorations could also be used on co-ordinating mini cakes

Recipes classic chocolate cake, chocolate buttercream

Techniques preparing cakes, using chocolate paste, using a sugar shaper, using cutters, using chocolate

winter wonderland

This snowy scene with cute carolling penguins would brighten up any Christmas table. Mum, dad and babies will bring smiles to the faces of all your guests, particularly the younger ones! This recipe uses a simple vanilla sponge cake, but you could use fruit cake or chocolate cake instead if you prefer. If you're feeling ambitious, you could make a larger cake and add some extra penguins!

All the models start from a simple ball. You can give your penguins their own personality by changing the colour of their clothes and facial expressions.

you will need ...

* ❋ 20cm (8in) round sponge cake
* ❋ 25cm (10in) round cake board
* ❋ 1kg 300g (2lb 14oz) white sugarpaste
* ❋ 200g (7oz) black sugarpaste
* ❋ 30g (1oz) orange sugarpaste
* ❋ 20g (¾oz) red sugarpaste
* ❋ 16g (½oz) green sugarpaste
* ❋ 1g (1/8oz) blue sugarpaste
* ❋ pale blue and pink dust food colour
* ❋ white paste food colour
* ❋ white vegetable fat (shortening)
* ❋ sugar glue
* ❋ 1cm (3/8in) and 5mm (1/8in) round cutters
* ❋ small Christmas tree cutter
* ❋ 1.5cm (½in) heart cutter
* ❋ blue ribbon: 15mm (½in) wide
* ❋ rice-textured rolling pin

1 Roll out 300g (10½oz) of white sugarpaste to 3mm (1/8in) and texture with a rice-textured rolling pin. Cover the board and trim the edges neatly.

2 Cover the cake with 600g (1lb 5oz) of white sugarpaste, rolled out to 5mm (1/8in), and trim the edges neatly. Attach the cake to the centre of the board using sugar glue and edge the board with blue ribbon.

3 Roll out 250g (8¾oz) of white sugarpaste into a strip measuring 6 x 70cm (2½ x 27½in) and texture with the rolling pin. Using a cutting wheel, shape the top into irregular peaks, making sure the beginning and end match in height.

4 Apply sugar glue around the cake base and attach the frieze, joining at the back. Allow the sugarpaste to dry before dusting the cake and board with pale blue dust food colour.

5 Using the leftover sugarpaste, cut out some trees using a small Christmas tree cutter. Vary the shapes of the trees in height, adding a tree trunk and make a taller tree from a simple triangle.

6 Attach the trees in groups at the front and back of the cake. Create a 3D effect by cutting out two trees, then cut the second tree in half and place in the middle of the first tree at a 90-degree angle.

the mother penguin ...

1 For the body, roll 58g (2oz) of black sugarpaste into a ball and then a cone shape. Pinch out a pointed tail at the back and place upright. Push a length of dry spaghetti through the centre leaving 2cm (¾in) at the top.

2 Make the feet using 12g (½oz) of orange sugarpaste equally divided. Make two cone shapes and flatten slightly, then indent two claw marks at the front and attach to the base of the body.

3 For the front of the body, roll out 12g (½oz) of white sugarpaste into a triangle shape. Attach to the front of the penguin, folding the lower edge under.

4 For the head, roll 20g (¾oz) of black sugarpaste into a ball and place inside a flower former. Indent across the centre where the cheeks will be attached.

5 For the cheeks and beak you will need 2g (¾oz) of orange sugarpaste. Take off a small amount for the beak and set it aside. Roll the remainder into a short sausage and narrow it in the centre.

6 Apply sugar glue across the face and attach the cheeks. Press the centre gently with your finger and then push a short piece of dry spaghetti into the middle.

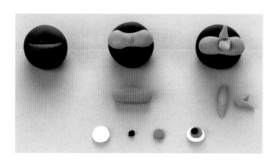

7 For the beak, roll a small sausage, making it pointed at both ends. Fold the shape in half lengthways and attach to the centre of the cheeks.

8 For the eyes, cut out two 1cm (³⁄₈in) circles in white sugarpaste and attach. Cut out two 5mm (¹⁄₈in) circles in blue sugarpaste and secure to the white circles. Roll two tiny black balls and attach these to the blue circles.

9 Highlight the eyes using white paste food colour on the tip of a cocktail stick, then blush the cheeks with pink dust food colour. Apply sugar glue around the neck and slip the head over the spaghetti.

10 To make the flippers, equally divide 12g (½oz) of black sugarpaste. Make a cone shape and flatten. Push a piece of spaghetti into the top of the body on either side. Apply sugar glue and attach the flippers in a bent position.

11 For the scarf you will need 10g (³⁄₈oz) of green sugarpaste rolled out to 1 x 24cm (³⁄₈ x 9½in). Fringe each end and wrap around the neck.

12 For the hat, take 6g (¼oz) of green sugarpaste and shape it into a pointed cone. Place the cone on to the work surface to flatten it, and hollow out the inside. Push dry spaghetti into the top of the head and add the hat.

13 Make a band for the hat using 2g (¹⁄₁₆oz) of white sugarpaste rolled out to a strip measuring 1 x 9cm (³⁄₈ x 3½in).

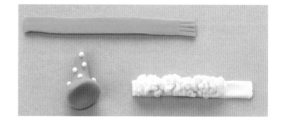

14 Fill the cup of a sugar shaper with 10g (³/₈oz) of white sugarpaste softened with white vegetable fat (shortening). Extrude short strands and attach them to the band then secure to the hat. Add some tiny white balls to the green part of the hat.

15 To make the book, roll and cut out a rectangle using 2g (¹/₁₆oz) of red sugarpaste to 1.5 x 3.5cm (½ x 1³/₈in). Cut out two slightly smaller rectangles using 2g (¹/₁₆oz) of white sugarpaste and attach them to the centre of the red cover.

16 Bend the book in half and mark two lines for the spine, then open the book and arrange the pages so they appear loose on the edges. Attach to the flippers with sugar glue and support with foam until dry.

the father penguin ...

1 Complete as for the mother penguin, but make the white front smaller than the mother's using 10g (³/₈oz) of white sugarpaste.

2 The song sheet is made from 5g (¹/₄oz) of white sugarpaste rolled out and cut to measure 4 x 3cm (1½ x 1¼in), then folded.

3 Make the red hat and scarf as for the green version, but using 16g (½oz) of red sugarpaste and with a ball attached to the hat instead of fringing. Make the hat band using 3g (¹/₈oz) of white sugarpaste rolled into a strip measuring 1 x 10cm (³/₈ x 4in).

the hatching penguin …

1 To complete all the baby penguins, mix 7g (¼oz) of black sugarpaste with 70g (2½oz) of white sugarpaste to make a pale grey shade.

2 To make the body of the hatching penguin, roll 6g (¼oz) of grey sugarpaste into a cone shape. Push a short piece of dry spaghetti into the rounded end for the head. Apply edible glue under the mother and attach the body.

3 To make the flippers, equally divide 1g (⅛oz) of grey sugarpaste. Make two small cone shapes and attach to the sides of the body.

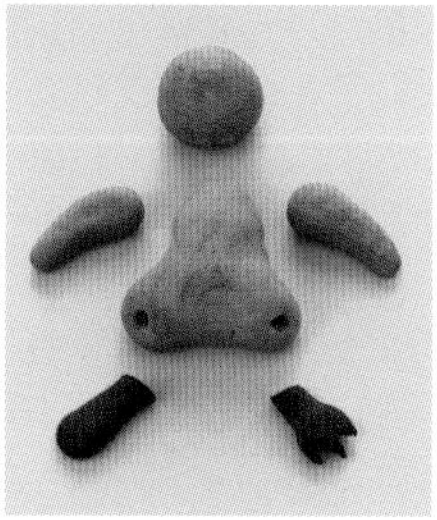

4 Make two small feet by equally dividing 1g (⅛oz) of black sugarpaste and rolling two cone shapes. Flatten slightly and cut out two 'V' shapes in each foot to form three claws. Attach underneath the body.

5 For the head, roll 2g (⅛oz) of grey sugarpaste into a small ball, apply some sugar glue around the neck and attach. For the face, roll out 2g (⅛oz) of white sugarpaste and cut using a 1.5cm (½in) heart cutter. Attach with sugar glue and push a short piece of dry spaghetti in the centre. Set the remainder aside for the cheeks.

6 Mark the eyes with the end of your paintbrush, making two small holes. Roll two tiny balls of black sugarpaste and place inside.

7 Make the beak in the same way as for the mother penguin. For the cheeks, add two small white balls on either side of the beak and dust with pink dust food colour.

the baby penguins ...

1 To complete each of the three baby penguins, take off 13g (½oz) of the grey sugarpaste and roll into a fat cone shape for the body.

2 Shape the leg area with your fingers and give each body a fat tummy with a small pointed tail. Push the end of your paintbrush into the end of the leg. Stand the body upright and push a piece of dry spaghetti down through centre, leaving 1cm (⅜in) at the top.

3 To make the feet, equally divide 1g (⅛oz) of black sugarpaste and roll two small cone shapes. Make as described for the hatching penguin, apply sugar glue inside the holes in the legs and insert the feet.

4 For the head, roll 6g (¼oz) of grey sugarpaste into a ball and slip it over the spaghetti at the neck. Make the face, eyes, beak and cheeks as described for the hatching penguin.

5 For the flippers, equally divide 2g (³⁄₆₀z) of grey sugarpaste and roll into flattened cone shapes. Push dry spaghetti into each side of the body and attach the flippers.

6 When dry, firmly attach the two large penguins to the top of the cake with sugar glue. Place one baby penguin at the side of the father penguin and the other two at the front.

Recipes traditional sponge cake, sugarpaste, sugar glue
Techniques preparing cakes, using sugarpaste, using cutters

all wrapped up

This fun design makes a show-stopping centrepiece, with a cute little gift box stacked on top of a wrapped present. Both are decorated with simple flower paste shapes to resemble Christmas wrapping paper. The classic red, white and green colour scheme gives this cake a traditional look, but you could use different colours to match your decorations or table settings.

The gorgeous bow at the top of the cake is made with strips of red flower paste. If you're short of time, you could make a simpler version using fewer strips of sugarpaste.

you will need ...

- ❋ 18cm (7in) square fruit cake
- ❋ 10cm (4in) square fruit cake
- ❋ 30cm (12in) round cake board
- ❋ 200g (7oz) white flower paste
- ❋ 200g (7oz) red flower paste
- ❋ royal icing
- ❋ sugar glue
- ❋ green and brown food colouring
- ❋ four hollow dowels
- ❋ small circle cutter
- ❋ holly cutter
- ❋ disposable piping (pastry) bag
- ❋ piping tubes (tips) nos. 1 plain, 4
- ❋ fine paintbrush
- ❋ white ribbon: 1.5cm (⅝in) wide
- ❋ double-sided tape

1 Cover the 30cm (12in) round cake board with white sugarpaste. Cover the 18cm (7in) square fruit cake with marzipan and red sugarpaste. Then cover the 10cm (4in) square fruit cake with marzipan and white sugarpaste.

2 Dowel the larger cake and stick it on the iced cake board with some stiff royal icing. Stick on the top tier and, using two icing smoothers, twist it so that it is at a different angle from the base cake.

3 To make the 'ribbon' trimming for the bottom tier, roll out some white flower paste thinly. Cut out four shaped strips about 15cm (6in) long and 2.5cm (1in) wide.

4 Place the strip at the bottom of the cake and drape it over the top to measure the correct length before you trim and stick it in position with sugar glue – it should come right up to the bottom of the top tier. Repeat this on all four sides of the cake.

5 To make the 'ribbon' trimming for the top tier, roll out four strips of red flower paste about 13cm (5in) long and 2cm (¾in) wide and stick them on the cake as in Step 4.

6 To decorate the bottom tier, roll out some white flower paste and cut out small circles using a circle cutter. Stick them to the cake with sugar glue so they are evenly spaced in a polka-dot fashion.

If the bases of your cakes are a little untidy, wrap some ribbon around them to neaten. Alternatively, fill in any cracks with watered-down sugarpaste

7 To decorate the top tier, colour 100g (1oz) of white flower paste with green food colouring and roll it out thinly. Cut holly shapes using the holly cutter and stick them to the cake with sugar glue. You will need to trim some of the shapes using a small, sharp knife where they meet the 'ribbon' trimming so that it looks as though the 'pattern' continues underneath.

8 Using a no. 4 piping tube (tip), cut out small circles for the berries from thinly rolled out red flower paste and stick them on to the holly sprigs. Paint the stems on the holly sprigs using a fine paintbrush and brown food colouring.

9 To make the pretty edging on the bottom tier ribbon, pipe small dots with soft-peak royal icing. Pipe the first row close to each other and touching the white band and then another row touching the first, but missing a space after each one.

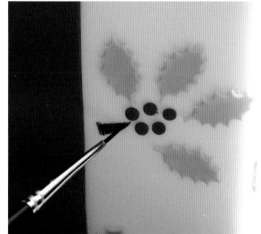

10 To make the bow, thinly roll out some red flower paste and cut strips about 12cm (4¾in) long and 2cm (¾in) wide. Make a loop and stick the two ends together with sugar glue, squeezing them in slightly. Turn it on its side to dry slightly. Repeat until you have 15–20 loops.

11 Stick the loops together to form the bow before they are all dry using sugar glue, then stick the bow to the top of the cake.

12 Finish by attaching the white satin ribbon around the cake board with double-sided tape.

If the loops are still a bit soft, use rolled-up pieces of kitchen paper (paper towel) in between them to hold them in position until they are dry

Recipes rich fruit cake, royal icing, sugarpaste, flower paste, sugar glue
Techniques preparing cakes, using sugarpaste, dowelling cakes, using royal icing, using cutters

Tasty Treats

fabulous firs

These ornate stencilled cupcakes look so elegant with white tree designs on bright green sugarpaste. You could try various seasonal colour combinations and different stencils to make each cupcake unique.

you will need ...

* chocolate cupcakes
* complementary flavour of syrup, alcohol, buttercream or ganache
* green sugarpaste
* 5mm ($^3/_{16}$in) spacers
* fluted circle cutter to fit the top of your cupcakes
* Christmas tree stencil
* royal icing
* superwhite dust

1 Brush the cupcakes with syrup or alcohol, or add a thin layer of buttercream or ganache to help the sugarpaste stick.

2 Knead the sugarpaste to warm, then roll out between the spacers.

3 Mix the superwhite dust into the royal icing to whiten it, and adjust the consistency of the icing – you need to have the icing fairly thick but still spreadable, so be prepared to add more icing sugar or water as necessary.

4 Place the stencil onto the sugarpaste and carefully spread the royal icing over the stencil. Once the icing is of an even thickness, remove the stencil, taking care not to smudge the pattern.

5 Cut out the tree patterns using the fluted circle cutter. Using a palette knife, lift a paste circle carefully onto each cupcake, easing the fullness in if necessary. Run your finger around the edge of each circle to smooth the sugarpaste.

Recipes classic chocolate cake, ganache, buttercream, sugarpaste, royal icing
Techniques preparing cakes, using sugarpaste, using royal icing

gingerbread scene

These cute cookies make great treats for children. The snow-topped house, smiley faces and red and white colour-scheme will appeal to all ages, and they're surprisingly easy to make.

you will need ...

* gingerbread cookie dough
* red sugarpaste
* mini quilting embosser
* gingerbread family and house cutters
* cutting wheel
* piping gel
* piping (pastry) bag
* piping tubes (tips) nos. 1.5, 3
* royal icing

1 Roll out the cookie dough. Cut out shapes using the gingerbread family and house cutters and bake.

2 Roll out the red sugarpaste to 3mm (⅛in). Emboss with the mini quilting embosser, taking care to line it up each time you repeat the pattern.

3 Cut out a gingerbread man using the cutter used to create the cookies. Take the cutting wheel and cut a waistcoat shape using the shape of the gingerbread man as a guide. Attach to the cookie using piping gel.

4 Repeat for the children, altering the shape of their clothing, and for the door of the house.

5 Fill a piping (pastry) bag with royal icing and attach the no. 1.5 piping tube (tip). Pipe around the outline of the cookies then add buttons, facial features and details. Use the no. 3 tube (tip) to add snow to the house.

Check the consistency of the icing before you start piping

Recipes   gingerbread, sugarpaste, royal icing, piping gel
Techniques   baking cookies, using sugarpaste, using royal icing, using cutters

we three kings

Inspired by the three wise men, these pretty cupcakes are bejewelled with glitter and shiny decorations to represent their gold, frankincense and myrrh offerings. Why not design your own crowns to add to the collection?

you will need ...

- ❋ vanilla cupcakes
- ❋ various colours of royal icing
- ❋ various colours of glacé icing
- ❋ small piping (pastry) bag and piping tube (tip)
- ❋ pink and blue shiny decoration balls
- ❋ edible glitter

1 Prepare all the cupcakes with different colours of glacé icing, spreading a neat disc to the edge of each cupcake.

2 Use a contrasting colour of royal icing to pipe coloured crowns on to each cupcake.

3 Finish with shiny decoration balls and edible glitter.

Make some starry night cupcakes to accompany your crown designs

Recipes traditional sponge cake, glacé icing, royal icing   ***Techniques*** preparing cakes, using royal icing

brilliant brownies

These festive parcels are a perfect treat for someone special at Christmas. Irresistible brownie squares are wrapped with decadent chocolate paste bows for a delicious result!

you will need ...

* brownies
* 50g (1¾oz) dark, milk and white chocolate paste
* 25g (1oz) dark couverture chocolate
* 25g white couverture chocolate
* disposable piping (pastry) bag and piping tube (tip)

1 To make the dark and milk chocolate bows, roll out the dark and milk chocolate paste and cut into 1cm (³⁄₈in) diameter strips.

2 Temper the dark chocolate and pipe a little onto the brownies to attach the chocolate paste strips.

3 Take two equal strips of paste and fold them over until they meet in the middle to form the bow. Attach bows to the brownies, then cut smaller pieces of paste to lay over the centre of the bows.

4 Temper 10g (¼oz) of white chocolate, place in a disposable piping (pastry) bag and carefully pipe tiny dots onto the bows.

For the white chocolate bows, create white chocolate paste strips and pipe dots using tempered dark chocolate

Recipes brownies *Techniques* using chocolate paste, using chocolate

winter frost

These delightful cupcakes, covered in white icing and topped with beautiful snowflakes will go with a flurry at any Christmas occasion. You can use different cutters and piping tubes (tips) to create endless snowflake designs.

you will need ...

❉ chocolate cupcakes
❉ royal icing
❉ snowflake cutters
❉ pastillage
❉ superwhite dust
❉ 1.5mm (¹/₁₆in) spacers
❉ small cutters and piping tubes (tips): nos. 4, 16 and 32R
❉ foam pads
❉ piping (pastry) bag, coupler and large star piping tube (tip)

1 Whiten the pastillage by kneading in superwhite dust. Roll out some of the pastillage between the spacers, then place it over a snowflake cutter.

2 Roll over the pastillage with a rolling pin. Run your finger over the edges of the cutter to achieve a clean cut. Turn the cutter over and carefully press out the pastillage.

3 Take either small cutters or piping tubes (tips) and remove a selection of shapes radiating out from the centre.

4 Once the pastillage has hardened, place on a foam pad and dry thoroughly (ideally overnight). An airing cupboard is an ideal place.

5 Place the star tube (tip) into a piping (pastry) bag and half fill with royal icing.

6 Pressure pipe the icing onto your cupcakes in the style of your choice and immediately insert a dried snowflake vertically into the soft icing on each cake.

Recipes classic chocolate cake, pastillage, royal icing
Techniques preparing cakes, using royal icing, using cutters

marzipan trees

These quirky little Christmas trees have a surprisingly traditional fruit cake and marzipan filling. They're easy to make and you can have fun creating your own patterns for each one.

you will need ...

* fruit cake, baked in dariole moulds
* marzipan
* white, red or green sugarpaste
* white, red and green flower paste
* piping tube (tip) no. 4
* holly cutter
* star cutter
* sugar glue

1 Form the marzipan into cones to fit the tops of the cakes.

2 Wrap thinly rolled-out white, red or green sugarpaste around the trees, trimming any excess. Blend the join by rubbing your finger along the edge. Add a contrasting sugarpaste strip around each base using sugar glue.

3 Decorate with flower paste holly sprigs, stars and small circles for the holly berries cut out with a no. 4 piping tube (tip).

As an alternative decoration, you could pipe designs on the mini cakes using royal icing

Recipes rich fruit cake, sugarpaste, flower paste, sugar glue
Techniques preparing cakes, using sugarpaste, using cutters

snowflake sensation

Beautifully decorated with snowflakes and a sparkling gem topper, these chocolate mini cakes look simply divine presented on a plate with raspberries or a scoop of your favourite ice cream. The perfect way to end your Christmas meal!

you will need ...

❊ 6 chocolate mini cakes: 4cm (1½in) high and 5cm (2in) in diameter

❊ 500g (1lb 2oz) dark chocolate

❊ 750g (1lb 10½oz) dark chocolate paste

❊ 300g (11oz) dark chocolate curls

❊ snowflake transfer sheet

❊ 6 flower gems

❊ 6 flower picks

1 Prepare the mini cakes and cover with dark chocolate paste.

2 Measure the circumference of the mini cakes. Calculate the area needed for the transfer sheet by adding an extra 2.5cm (1in) to the height and 2cm (¾in) to the width of the cakes to allow for an overlap, then cut out.

3 Temper the dark chocolate and pour onto the rough side of the transfer sheet. Use a palette knife to spread the chocolate evenly across the sheet.

4 After a minute, wrap the transfer sheet around a mini cake, allowing it to overlap at the back. Repeat this process for all of the mini cakes.

5 Place the cakes in the fridge for 20 minutes or until set. Remove the backing from the transfer sheet to reveal the snowflake pattern.

6 Insert a small flower pick into the centre of each cake, fill with a little dark chocolate paste and place the flower gem into the pick. Fill the top of the cakes with dark chocolate curls.

Recipes classic chocolate cake *Techniques* preparing cakes, using chocolate paste, using chocolate

Delicious Decorations

beautiful baubles

These sparkling decorations look just like the real thing – and they taste great too! Use them to adorn your Christmas tree or hang them around the house to brighten up every room.

you will need ...

❋ vanilla cookie dough

❋ various colours of sugarpaste

❋ bauble cutters

❋ piping gel

❋ royal icing

❋ piping (pastry) bag and piping tubes (tips) nos. 2, 18

❋ edible snowflake lustre dust

❋ white hologram disco dust

❋ soft brush

1 Roll out the cookie dough and cut out shapes using the bauble cutters. Remove a small circle of dough from the top of the cookies using a no. 18 piping tube (tip) and bake.

2 Roll out the sugarpaste and cut shapes using the bauble cutters. Attach to the cookies using piping gel. Remove a circle using the no. 18 tube (tip) to reveal the hole in each cookie.

3 Fill a piping (pastry) bag with royal icing, attach the no. 2 tube (tip) and pipe a design over the cookies.

4 Once the royal icing has set, mix some lustre dust with water and paint over the pattern. Then spread white hologram dust over the cookies with a soft brush.

5 Thread metallic cord through the hole in each cookie and tie to form a loop.

Be creative with your designs, using different colours and patterns to create unique baubles

Recipes vanilla cookies, sugarpaste, royal icing, piping gel
Techniques baking cookies, using sugarpaste, using royal icing, using cutters

snowy stockings

These stocking cookies will add colour and fun to your tree this Christmas. These instructions are for the snowman design, but you can use the same techniques for a range of festive patterns.

you will need ...

* vanilla cookie dough
* black, white, red, green and orange sugarpaste
* stocking cutter
* royal icing
* piping gel
* snowman and tree cutters
* piping (pastry) bag and piping tubes (tips) nos. 2, 18

1 Roll out the cookie dough and cut out shapes using a stocking cutter. Remove a small circle of dough from the top of the cookies using a no. 18 piping tube (tip) and bake.

2 Roll out the green and red sugarpaste to 3mm (⅛in). Cut out a stocking from each colour using the cutter. Cut across the top of each stocking and attach the red and green pieces to the cookies using piping gel. Remove a circle from the green piece to reveal the hole in the top of each cookie.

3 Thinly roll out the white, black and green sugarpastes, adding gum tragacanth for firmness if desired.

4 Emboss snowmen into each colour of paste and use a craft knife to cut along the embossed lines of the shapes. Attach the appropriate sections of paste to the cookie and trim to fit. Add an orange nose. Make the tree in the same way and attach, then decorate with stars and baubles.

5 Pipe a row of royal iced dots on to the green stocking top and the tree.

Recipes vanilla cookies, sugarpaste, royal icing, pastillage, piping gel
Techniques baking cookies, using sugarpaste, using royal icing, using cutters

treasure trove

Christmas wouldn't be the same without a handful of chocolate pennies. Wrap them in gift bags with bright ribbons, hang them from the tree or use them as stocking fillers – children won't be able to resist!

you will need ...

* 100g (3½oz) tempered chocolate of your choice
* coin mould
* assorted foils
* disposable piping (pastry) bag

1 Polish the coin mould before use with a piece of kitchen paper (paper towel). Temper the chocolate and place in a piping (pastry) bag. Cut the end off the bag and fill the mould with chocolate.

2 Gently tap the mould against your work surface to bring any bubbles to the surface and allow the tempered chocolate to settle.

3 Place the mould in the fridge for 20 minutes to set. Once the chocolate has hardened, remove from the mould and wrap in coloured foil.

Why not add some peppermint essence to create tasty after-dinner mints

Techniques using chocolate

cookie crackers

Why not adorn your table with these glittering gold cracker-shaped cookies. They are easy to bake, fun to decorate, and are sure to create a bang with your guests! Alter the colours to suit your table decorations.

you will need ...

* gingerbread cookie dough
* gold, red and burgundy sugarpaste
* cracker cutter
* cutting wheel
* Dresden tool
* edible gold lustre dust
* confectioners' glaze
* piping tubes (tips) nos. 16, 18
* piping gel
* small circle cutter

1 Roll out the cookie dough and cut out shapes using a cracker cutter. To make the pulled cracker, cut a zigzag line through the central section. Separate the two halves and bake.

2 Cover each cracker with gold sugarpaste. For the pulled cracker, place the sugarpaste on the cookie and trim the zigzag section to shape.

3 Use a cutting wheel to mark four curved outside edges of the gathered sections on each cookie. Indent radial gathers using a Dresden tool.

4 Mix edible gold lustre dust with confectioners' glaze and paint over the gold sugarpaste to add extra sparkle. Allow to dry.

5 Thinly roll out the red and burgundy sugarpaste. Cut thin strips of paste and attach to the centre of the gathered sections to create bows with piping gel.

6 Cut circles of sugarpaste using the cutter and piping tubes (tips). Attach to the crackers to create patterns.

Recipes gingerbread, sugarpaste, piping gel *Techniques* baking cookies, using sugarpaste, using cutters

chocolate drops

These hanging treats will look great on your tree and the variations are endless. Get creative and experiment with shapes, patterns and ribbons or even present some in a gift box for a melt-in-the-mouth festive surprise.

you will need ...

* 1kg (2lb 3oz) white chocolate

* two transfer sheets: holly, red gingham

* metal round cutters: 6.5cm (2½in) and 1cm (³/₈in) in diameter

* metal holly cutter

* gold ribbon: 3mm (¹/₈in) wide

1 Temper the white chocolate and spread an even layer onto the rough, patterned side of the holly and red gingham transfer sheets.

2 Wait a few minutes until the chocolate begins to dull. Use the large round cutter and holly cutter to carefully cut shapes out of the chocolate, making sure that the transfer sheets are kept in place.

3 Use the small round cutter to cut out a disc at the top of each shape.

4 Place the chocolate in the fridge for 20 minutes, or until firm. Once the chocolate is set, carefully remove the backing from the transfer sheets. Tie decorative ribbon through the small round holes and hang from the tree.

You could use dark chocolate instead of white chocolate with coloured transfer patterns to suit

Techniques using cutters, using chocolate

mistletoe magic

Sure to be a hit at any Christmas party, lift up the little mistletoe plaque for your Christmas kisses. The pearlescent decoration balls and decadent buttercream add a touch of class to these festive treats.

you will need ...

❄ vanilla cupcakes

❄ buttercream

❄ disposable piping (pastry) bag with fine star tube (tip)

❄ flower paste

❄ mistletoe stencil

❄ royal icing

❄ green colouring

❄ mother of pearl decoration balls

1 Roll out the flower paste and cut out small squares, or different shapes if you like, and allow to harden off.

2 Place the mistletoe stencil on each flower paste plaque and apply a small quantity of stiff green royal icing across the stencil with a palette knife to create the mistletoe picture.

3 Pipe a generous swirl of buttercream on each cupcake. Place plaques on the cupcakes and complete by adding mother of pearl decoration balls for the mistletoe berries.

Why not use these cupcakes as a stylish alternative to place cards for a table setting

Recipes traditional sponge cake, buttercream, flower paste, royal icing
Techniques preparing cakes, using sugarpaste, using buttercream

Perfect Presents

pretty parcels

These mini cakes are bright and fun. Decorated with large spotty bows, they are inspired by all those wonderfully colourful Christmas papers, ribbons and trimmings used to wrap your presents!

you will need ...

* ❄ vanilla mini cakes
* ❄ white, red, green and yellow sugarpaste
* ❄ piping gel
* ❄ piping tube (tip) no. 3
* ❄ small round cutter
* ❄ no. 12 stitch marking tool
* ❄ 4cm (1½in) and 1cm (³⁄₈in) star cutters

1 Roll out some white sugarpaste and cover the mini cakes.

2 Roll out the red, green and yellow sugarpastes and trim into thin strips. Use any excess sugarpaste to cut out circles using the small round cutter.

3 Wrap two long strips of sugarpaste around each mini cake. Then stick two shorter pieces diagonally on top. Create two loops of sugarpaste and wrap a thin strip around them to complete the bow. Attach the small circles to the bows.

4 For the star decorations cut out 4cm (1½in) star shapes from the white sugarpaste and using a small 1cm (³⁄₈in) star-shaped cutter, take out the centres. Using tool no. 12, mark with stitch marks from the top of each point to the centre. Make small holes using a no. 3 piping tube (tip). Push into the top of each bow.

For a quicker finish, leave the bows plain and remove the star decorations

Recipes traditional sponge cake, sugarpaste, piping gel
Techniques preparing cakes, using sugarpaste, using cutters

star of wonder

Your family and friends will love these bitesize chocolate treats. To make them unique, you could pipe a design on to each one with royal icing. Tie a stack together with organza ribbon for a tasty stocking filler.

you will need ...

* chocolate bites, 6cm (2³⁄₈in) in diameter
* 250g (9oz) white chocolate paste
* 25g (1oz) dark couverture chocolate
* large star cutter
* disco white hologram edible cake glitter
* red dusting spray
* disposable piping (pastry) bag and piping tube (tip)

1 Prepare a batch of chocolate bites. Evenly roll out 250g (9oz) of white chocolate paste onto icing (confectioners') sugar and use the large star cutter to cut out 9 star shapes.

2 Spray some of the white chocolate paste stars with the red dusting spray and dust the remainder with the disco white hologram edible cake glitter.

3 Temper 25g (1oz) of dark couverture chocolate and place in a disposable piping (pastry) bag. Pipe a small dot of chocolate onto the top of the chocolate bites and position a star on top. Pipe another dot of chocolate onto this star and arrange the second star on top, using different colours if desired.

Easy to make without any baking required, you can indulge by varying the size of your bites

Recipes chocolate bites *Techniques* using chocolate paste, using cutters, using chocolate

candy cane treats

These fun and bright cookies work well as tree decorations or festive place settings – just tie a ribbon around each candy cane and attach a label with each guest's name!

you will need ...

- ❅ chocolate cookie dough
- ❅ white and red sugarpaste
- ❅ piping gel
- ❅ candy cane cutter
- ❅ tiny circle cutter (optional)
- ❅ narrow ribbon, for hanging or tying (optional)

1 Roll out the cookie dough. Cut out shapes using a candy cane cutter and bake.

2 Roll out the white sugarpaste, cut with the candy cane cutter and fix to the cookie using piping gel.

3 Cut thin strips of red sugarpaste and lay over each cookie to create a striped pattern. Attach to the white sugarpaste and trim the edges for a neat finish.

4 If you want to hang the cookies, carefully cut a small hole at the top with a tiny circle cutter as soon as they come out of the oven when the dough is still soft. Thread the holes with narrow ribbon, or tie ribbon around the cookies if you prefer.

Chocolate cookie dough is used here, but gingerbread or vanilla cookies would be equally as delicious

Recipes chocolate cookies, sugarpaste, piping gel
Techniques baking cookies, using sugarpaste, using cutters

tempting truffles

Celebrate in style at Christmas with these sumptuous chocolate truffles. They are quick to create, utterly delicious and could be presented in a box or bag as an enticing festive gift to someone special.

you will need ...

* truffles
* 50g (1¾oz) dark couverture chocolate
* 25g (1oz) white couverture chocolate
* disposable piping (pastry) bag and piping tube (tip)
* acetate sheet

1 Prepare the truffles and allow to harden on a greaseproof sheet

2 Temper the dark couverture chocolate and dip the balls into the tempered chocolate. Remove the balls with a fork and tap them onto the edge of the bowl to remove any excess chocolate and air bubbles.

3 Place the truffles onto an acetate sheet and leave to dry for approximately 30 minutes.

4 Temper the white couverture chocolate, place in a disposable piping (pastry) bag and drizzle over the truffles. Leave for ten minutes, or until dry.

Instead of piping the truffles with white chocolate, try dipping them in a bowl of coconut or chopped nuts before the dark chocolate covering dries

Recipes truffles   *Techniques* using chocolate

festive fancies

These cupcakes are guaranteed to bring a burst of happiness and cheer at Christmas. Show off your seasonal flare by varying the colours and shapes to make each one a unique treat for your family and friends.

you will need ...

* vanilla cupcakes
* complementary flavour of syrup, alcohol, buttercream or ganache
* assorted colours of sugarpaste
* 5mm (³/₁₆in) spacers
* set of circle and square cutters
* piping (pastry) bag and tubes (tips) nos. 18, 16 and 4

1 Brush the cakes with sugar syrup or alcohol, or add a thin layer of buttercream or ganache to help the sugarpaste stick to the cakes.

2 Knead the sugarpaste, then roll it out between the spacers. Cut out one circle to cover each cake, using a large circle cutter.

3 Using a palette knife, lift a paste circle carefully onto each cupcake. Run your finger around the edge of each circle to smooth the sugarpaste.

4 Roll out the different colours of sugarpaste to a thickness of 5mm (³/₁₆in). Cut out a selection of circles and squares of varying sizes.

5 Decorate the cupakes with sugarpaste shapes and top each one with a ball of sugarpaste.

Use a small paintbrush and some water to stick the shapes in place

Recipes traditional sponge cake, ganache, sugarpaste, buttercream
Techniques preparing cakes, using sugarpaste, using cutters

heavenly angel

These cookies are easy and fun to create, so why not bake them for your own little angels at Christmas? You could use them to adorn your Christmas tree or they make perfect treats at a Christmas party.

you will need ...

* vanilla cookie dough
* angel cutter
* assorted colours of sugarpaste
* Dresden tool
* piping gel

1 Roll out the cookie dough. Cut out shapes using an angel cutter and bake.

2 Roll out the coloured sugarpastes and cut using the cutter used to create the cookies. Attach to the cookie using piping gel.

3 Use a Dresden tool to add texture to the wings and dress. The angels' hair can be created using a sugar shaper fitted with a mesh disc.

Make simple star cookies covered with colourful sugarpaste to accompany your little angels

---

Recipes vanilla cookies, sugarpaste **Techniques** baking cookies, using sugarpaste, using a sugar shaper

recipes

traditional sponge cake

For a really light sponge cake, it's better to separate the mixture between two tins. If you want a three-layer cake, split the mixture one-third/two-thirds. For smaller cakes, you can also cut three layers of sponge from a larger square cake.

1 Preheat your oven to 160°C/325°F/Gas Mark 3 and line your tins.

2 In a large electric mixer, beat the butter and sugar together until light and fluffy. Meanwhile, crack your eggs into a separate bowl. Add the eggs gradually, beating well between each addition. Then add the vanilla extract.

3 Sift the flour, add to the mixture and mix carefully until just combined.

Make sure that the butter and eggs you are using are at room temperature before you start

4 Remove the mixing bowl from the mixer and fold the mixture gently with a spatula to finish. Tip it into your prepared tins and spread with a palette knife or the back of a spoon.

5 Bake in the oven until a skewer inserted into the centre of your cakes comes out clean. The baking time will vary depending on your oven. Check small cakes after 20 minutes and larger cakes after 40 minutes.

6 Allow to cool, then wrap in cling film and refrigerate until ready to use.

Cake size	13cm (5in) round 10cm (4in) square 10–12 cupcakes	18cm (7in) round 15.5cm (6in) square 16 x 5cm (2in) mini cakes	20cm (8in) round 18cm (7in) square	23cm (9in) round 20cm (8in) square
Unsalted butter	150g (5½oz)	250g (9oz)	325g (11½oz)	450g (1lb)
Caster (superfine) sugar	150g (5½oz)	250g (9oz)	325g (11½oz)	450g (1lb)
Medium eggs	3	5	6	9
Self-raising (-rising) flour	150g (5½oz)	250g (9oz)	325g (11½oz)	450g (1lb)
Vanilla extract	½ tsp	1 tsp	1½ tsp	2 tsp

classic chocolate cake

This recipe is quick and easy to make and has a lovely light texture. You should split the cake mixture between two tins, either dividing it equally or into one-third and two-thirds for a three-layered cake.

1 Preheat your oven to 160°C/325°F/Gas Mark 3 and line your tins.

2 Sift the flour, cocoa powder (unsweetened cocoa) and baking powder together.

3 In a large electric mixer, beat the butter (at room temperature) and sugar together until light and fluffy. Then crack your eggs into a separate bowl.

4 Add the eggs to the mixture gradually, beating well between each addition.

5 Add half the dry ingredients and mix until just combined before adding half the milk. Repeat with the remaining ingredients and mix until they start to combine.

For a chocolate orange variation, add the finely grated zest of one orange per two eggs used

6 Finish mixing by hand with a spatula and then spoon into your prepared tins.

7 Bake in the oven until a skewer inserted into the centre of your cakes comes out clean. The baking time will vary depending on your oven. Check smaller cakes after 20 minutes and larger cakes after 40 minutes.

8 Leave to cool, then wrap in cling film and refrigerate until ready to use.

Cake size	13cm (5in) round 10cm (4in) square 10–12 cupcakes	18cm (7in) round 15.5cm (6in) square 16 x 5cm (2in) mini cakes	20cm (8in) round 18cm (7in) square	23cm (9in) round 20cm (8in) square
Plain (all-purpose) flour	170g (6oz)	280g (10oz)	365g (12½oz)	500g (1lb 2oz)
Cocoa powder (unsweetened cocoa)	30g (1oz)	50g (1¾oz)	65g (2¼oz)	90g (3¼oz)
Baking powder	1½ tsp	2½ tsp	3¼ tsp	4½ tsp
Unsalted butter	150g (5½oz)	250g (9oz)	325g (11½oz)	450g (1lb)
Caster (superfine) sugar	130g (4½oz)	220g (8oz)	285g (10oz)	400g (14oz)
Large eggs	2½	4	5	7
Full-fat (whole) milk	100ml (3½fl oz)	170ml (5¾fl oz)	220ml (8fl oz)	300ml (10fl oz)

rich fruit cake

With this recipe, ideally your cake should be baked at least one month before it is eaten to allow it time to mature. You need to soak your dried fruit and mixed peel in the alcohol at least 24 hours in advance.

1 Preheat your oven to 150°C/300°F/Gas Mark 2 and line your tin with two or three layers of greaseproof paper or baking parchment.

2 In a large electric mixer, beat the butter and sugar together with the lemon and orange zest until light and fluffy. Add the orange juice to the soaked fruit and mixed peel.

3 Gradually add your eggs, one at a time, beating well after each. Sift the flour and spices together and add half the flour mixture plus half the soaked fruit mixture to the cake mixture. Mix until just combined then add the remaining flour and fruit.

4 Fold in the almonds and treacle (molasses) by hand, then spoon into your prepared baking tin. Cover the top loosely with greaseproof paper and bake in the oven for the time indicated or until a skewer inserted into the centre comes out clean.

5 Pour more alcohol over the cake while it's hot and leave to cool in the tin. Once cool, remove from the tin and wrap in a layer of greaseproof paper and then foil to store.

Cake size	13cm (5in) round 10cm (4in) square	18cm (7in) round 15.5cm (6in) square 16 x 5cm (2in) mini cakes	20cm (8in) round 18cm (7in) square	23cm (9in) round 20cm (8in) square
Currants	125g (4½oz)	225g (8oz)	300g (10½oz)	375g (13oz)
Raisins	150g (5½oz)	275g (9½oz)	350g (12oz)	450g (1lb)
Sultanas (golden raisins)	150g (5½oz)	275g (9½oz)	350g (12oz)	450g (1lb)
Glacé (candied) cherries	50g (1¾oz)	100g (3½oz)	125g (4½oz)	150g (5½oz)
Mixed peel	30g (1oz)	50g (1¾oz)	70g (2½oz)	85g (3oz)
Brandy (or other alcohol)	2½ tbsp	3½ tbsp	5 tbsp	6 tbsp
Slightly salted butter	125g (4½oz)	225g (8oz)	350g (12oz)	375g (13oz)
Brown sugar	125g (4½oz)	225g (8oz)	350g (12oz)	375g (13oz)
Grated zest of lemon (per fruit)	½	1	1½	1¾
Grated zest of orange (per fruit)	½	1	1½	1¾
Juice of orange (per fruit)	¼	½	¾	¾
Medium eggs	2½	4	6	7
Plain (all-purpose) flour	125g (4½oz)	225g (8oz)	350g (12oz)	375g (13oz)
Mixed (apple pie) spice	½ tsp	¾ tsp	1 tsp	1¼ tsp
Ground nutmeg	¼ tsp	½ tsp	½ tsp	¾ tsp
Ground almonds	15g (½oz)	25g (1oz)	35g (1¼oz)	45g (1½ oz)
Flaked (slivered) almonds	15g (½oz)	25g (1oz)	35g (1¼oz)	45g (1½ oz)
Black treacle (molasses)	¾ tbsp	1½ tbsp	1½ tbsp	1¾ tbsp
Baking time (hours)	2¾	3½	4	4½

vanilla cookies

Here is a recipe for delicious cookies that are sure to be adored by all. The cookies have a two-week shelf life so don't be afraid to start your baking well in advance.

you will need ...

* 275g (10oz) plain (all-purpose) flour
* 5ml (1 tsp) baking powder
* 100g (3½ oz) caster (superfine) sugar
* 75g (3oz) butter, diced
* 1 small egg, beaten
* 30ml (2 tbsp) golden syrup
* 2.5ml (½ tsp) vanilla extract

1 Preheat the oven to 170°C/325°F/ Gas Mark 3.

2 Place the dry ingredients in a mixing bowl. Add the butter and rub together with your fingertips until the mixture resembles fine breadcrumbs.

3 Make a hollow in the centre and pour in the beaten egg, golden syrup and vanilla extract. Mix together well, until you have a ball of dough. Place the dough in a plastic bag and chill in the refridgerator for 30 minutes.

4 Roll the dough out on a lightly floured surface to 5mm (³/₁₆in) thick and cut out your chosen shapes. Place the cookies on greased baking sheets.

5 Bake for 12–15 minutes until lightly coloured and firm but not crisp. Leave on the tray for two minutes before transferring to a wire rack to cool.

chocolate cookies ...

For an alternative cookie flavour, substitute 50g (1¾oz) of flour with cocoa powder (unsweetened cocoa).

gingerbread

Try this tasty recipe for gingerbread as an alternative to the vanilla-flavoured cookies. For gingerbread people you could try adding currants for eyes before baking.

you will need ...

* 125g (4oz) butter
* 60ml (4 tbsp) black treacle
* 225g (8oz) soft brown sugar
* 450g (1lb) plain (all-purpose) flour
* 15ml (1 tbsp) ground ginger
* 7.5ml (1½ tsp) cinnamon
* 5ml (1 tsp) bicarbonate of soda
* 15ml (1 tbsp) milk

1 Preheat the oven to 170°C/ 325°F/ Gas Mark 3.

2 Place the butter, treacle and sugar in a saucepan and heat gently until the sugar has dissolved and the butter melted. Cool slightly.

3 Sieve the dry ingredients into a mixing bowl. Pour the melted mixture into the dry ingredients and stir.

4 Dissolve the bicarbonate of soda in the milk and add to the mixture. Combine to make a dough, adding more milk if necessary.

5 Place the dough in a plastic bag and chill in the fridge for 40 minutes.

6 Continue as per steps 4–5 for cookies then bake for 10–15 minutes.

Mix the dry ingredients together thoroughly before mixing in the liquids

chocolate bites

These chocolate bites are so simple to make, don't require baking and taste sensational. You can choose to present them as they are or decorate them in a variety of ways.

you will need ...

* 12 digestive biscuits
* 250g (9oz) white, milk or dark chocolate
* 55g (2oz) butter
* 60ml (4 tbsp) drinking chocolate
* 30ml (2 tbsp) golden syrup
* 18cm (7in) tin
* round, metal cookie cutters

1 Melt the butter and golden syrup in a pan over a low heat. Add the drinking chocolate.

2 Crush the digestive biscuits in a bag with a rolling pin. Add the melted mixture to the biscuits. Push the mixture into the tin until it is flat and chill for approximately 20 minutes.

3 Temper the chocolate, pour onto the mixture and spread into an even layer using a palette knife. Tap the tin to remove any air bubbles and leave for approximately 10 minutes at room temperature until the mixture is partially set.

4 Use round metal cutters to cut out the bites. Leave to harden before decorating.

Do not let the chocolate set completely, or it will be difficult to cut out the individual bites

brownies

These tried and tested brownies will melt-in-the-mouth and delight any serious chocoholics! They can be decorated with sugarpaste, chocolate paste or royal icing for stylish results.

you will need ...

❋ 175g (6oz) caster (superfine) sugar

❋ 65g (2½oz) butter

❋ 65g (2½oz) self-raising (-rising) flour

❋ 55g (2oz) Belgian dark chocolate buttons or grated chocolate

❋ 2 eggs

❋ 18cm (7in) square tin

1 Pre-heat the oven to 180°C/350°F/Gas Mark 4. Grease and line the tin.

2 Melt the butter and chocolate in a microwave at full power (850w) for approximately 20 seconds, or over a pan of hot water.

3 Stir in the caster (superfine) sugar and sift in the flour, then add the melted chocolate, sugar, butter and eggs to the mixture.

4 Beat the mixture until smooth and pour into the tin. Bake in the oven for approximately 35 minutes.

5 Remove from the oven, allow to cool, then cut into 6 x 6cm (2⅜ x 2⅜in) squares using a sharp knife.

walnut brownies ...

If desired, add 55g (2oz) of walnut pieces after beating, remembering first to check if any recipients have a nut allergy

truffles

These delicious truffles are a perfect indulgence at Christmas. Experiment by using white, milk or dark chocolate ganache and adding flavourings to the mixture.

you will need ...

* one batch of ganache
* tempered couverture chocolate or cocoa powder (unsweetened cocoa)

1 Prepare the ganache and allow to cool for about 30 minutes at room temperature.

2 Make 15 balls approximately 2½cm (1in) in diameter by rolling strips of ganache. Place the balls on a greaseproof sheet and allow to harden completely.

Dip the truffles in tempered chocolate or roll in cocoa powder (unsweetened cocoa) to finish

Try adding a few drops of flavouring for a unique taste

ganache

Ganache is a delicious variety of icing that can be used to fill chocolates, chocolate truffles and other desserts. It can be used as an alternative to chocolate buttercream to fill a cake, or can be poured over a cake that has already had a thin coating of chocolate paste. Use the best dark chocolate you can source to ensure a really indulgent topping.

you will need ...

* 180ml (6fl oz) double (heavy) cream
* 200g (7oz) dark chocolate
* 25g (1oz) butter

1 Heat the cream and butter and pour over the chopped, dark chocolate.

2 Stir or blend the mixture until smooth. If desired, the mixture can be enhanced with liqueurs or extracts.

Be careful not to overheat the ganache or it may melt the chocolate cases

You could add 2 tsp of brandy or gin to the mixture to flavour the ganache

buttercream

Buttercream can be used as a delicious filling between cake layers, as a topping for cupcakes and mini cakes, or simply as a base for attaching decorations to your creations. It can be stored in a fridge for up to three weeks. Cover with cling film to prevent it from drying out.

you will need ...

* 100g (3½oz) unsalted butter
* 200g (7oz) icing (confectioners') sugar
* 15ml (1 tbsp) milk or water
* a few drops of vanilla extract or flavouring of your choice

1 Place the butter in a bowl and beat until light and fluffy.

2 Sift the icing (confectioners') sugar into the bowl and continue to beat until the mixture changes colour.

3 Add just enough milk or water to give a firm but spreadable consistency.

4 Flavour by adding the vanilla or alternative flavouring, then store the buttercream in an airtight container in a fridge until required. Re-beat before using.

Use white vegetable fat (shortening) instead of butter to achieve a pure white buttercream

chocolate buttercream ...
For a rich chocolate flavour, stir in 90g (3¼oz) of melted white, milk or dark (semisweet) chocolate

royal icing

Use royal icing for stencil work and to pipe fine detail. It is best used when fresh, but it will keep for up to five days in an airtight container. Rebeat the mixture before use if necessary.

you will need ...

❋ 1 egg white

❋ 250g (9oz) icing (confectioners') sugar, sieved

1 Lightly beat the egg white in a bowl. Gradually beat in the icing (confectioners') sugar until the icing is glossy and forms soft peaks.

2 Royal icing can be made in advance and stored, but mustn't be allowed to dry out. Store in the refrigerator in an airtight container and discard any crusted areas before using. If it is too stiff after storage it can be re-beaten to soften it up.

glacé icing ...
If you want to keep things simple, glacé icing is quick and easy to make. Sieve 300g (10½oz) icing (confectioners') sugar into a bowl and gradually beat in 2–4 tablespoons (30–60ml) of water a little at a time to give a thick, smooth texture.

sugarpaste (rolled fondant)

Sugarpaste is a sweet, thick, opaque paste that is soft, pliable, easily coloured and extremely versatile. Ready-made sugarpaste can be bought from supermarkets and cake-decorating suppliers, and is available in the whole colour spectrum. It is also easy and inexpensive to make your own.

you will need ...

* 60ml (4 tbsp) cold water
* 20ml (4 tsp) powdered gelatine
* 125ml (4fl oz) liquid glucose
* 15ml (1 tbsp) glycerine
* 1kg (2¼lb) icing (confectioners') sugar, sieved, plus extra for dusting

1 Place the water in a small bowl, sprinkle over the gelatine and soak until spongy.

2 Stand the bowl over a pan of hot, but not boiling, water and stir until the gelatine is dissolved. Add the glucose and glycerine, stirring until well blended and runny.

3 Put the icing (confectioners') sugar in a bowl. Make a well in the centre and slowly pour in the liquid ingredients, stirring constantly.

4 Turn out on to a surface dusted with icing (confectioners') sugar and knead until smooth, sprinkling with extra icing (confectioners') sugar if the paste becomes too sticky. The paste can be used immediately or wrapped and stored until required.

Store sugarpaste in thick plastic bags in an airtight container

flower paste (petal/gum paste)

Available commercially from sugarcraft suppliers, flower paste can be bought in white and a range of colours. There are many varieties available so try a few to see which you prefer. Alternatively, it is possible to make your own, but it is a time-consuming process and you will need a heavy-duty mixer.

you will need ...

* 500g (1lb 2oz) icing (confectioners') sugar
* 15ml (1 tbsp) gum tragacanth
* 25ml (1½ tbsp) cold water
* 10ml (2 tsp) powdered gelatine
* 10ml (2 tsp) liquid glucose
* 15ml (1 tbsp) white vegetable fat (shortening)
* 1 medium egg white

1 Sieve the icing (confectioners') sugar and gum tragacanth into the greased mixing bowl of a heavy-duty mixer (the grease eases the strain on the mixer).

2 Place the water in a small bowl, sprinkle over the gelatine and soak until spongy.

3 Stand the bowl over a pan of hot (but not boiling) water and stir until the gelatine has dissolved. Add the glucose and white fat to the gelatine and continue heating until all the ingredients are melted and mixed.

4 Add the glucose mixture and egg white to the icing (confectioners') sugar. Beat the mixture slowly until mixed, then increase the speed until the paste becomes white and stringy.

5 Grease your hands and remove the paste from the bowl. Stretch it several times and then knead together. Place in a plastic bag and store in an airtight container. Leave to mature for at least 12 hours.

pastillage

This is an extremely useful paste because, unlike other pastes, it sets extremely hard. It is not affected by moisture the way other pastes are, and it is used in this book to make decorations that are inserted into the cupcakes. Be aware, however, that the paste crusts quickly and is brittle once dry. You can buy it in a powdered form, to which you add water, but it is easy to make yourself.

you will need ...

* 1 egg white
* 300g (11oz) icing (confectioners') sugar, sifted
* 10ml (2 tsp) gum tragacanth

1 Put the egg white into a large mixing bowl. Gradually add enough icing (confectioners') sugar until the mixture combines together.

2 Mix in the gum tragacanth, and then turn the paste out on to a work board or work surface and knead the pastillage well.

3 Incorporate the remaining icing (confectioners') sugar into the remainder of the pastillage to give a stiff paste.

4 Store pastillage in a polythene bag placed in an airtight container in a refrigerator. Use within one month.

confectioner's glaze ...

This is available from cake decorating suppliers and can be used to add a glossy sheen. Mix it with edible lustre dust to create metallic edible paint.

piping gel

This is a multi-purpose transparent gel that is excellent for attaching sugarpaste. It can also add shimmering accents and colourful highlights. It is available commercially but is just as easy to make, using the following recipe. Once cooled it can be stored for up to two months.

you will need ...

* 15ml (1 tbsp) powdered gelatine

* 15ml (1 tbsp) cold water

* 250ml (9fl oz/1 cup) light corn syrup or liquid glucose

1 Sprinkle the gelatine over the cold water in a small saucepan and soak until spongy – about five minutes.

2 Heat on low until the gelatine has become clear and dissolved. Do not allow to boil.

3 Add syrup or glucose and heat thoroughly. Cool and store.

sugar glue ...

Although commercially available, sugar glue is quick and cheap to make at home. It is used for attaching pieces of sugarpaste to each other. To make, break up pieces of sugarpaste into a small container and cover with a little boiling water. Stir until dissolved. This produces a thick glue, which can be thinned easily by adding some more cooled boiled water.

techniques

preparing cakes

Preparing a cake for icing is a key process in achieving a smooth and perfectly shaped cake. The cutting, filling and coating of the cake needs to be done correctly to achieve a professional, even finish. Sponge cakes usually consist of two or three layers, but fruit cakes are kept whole.

cutting ...

Cut the dark-baked crust from the base of your cakes. You should have baked your cake 2.5cm (1in) larger all round than required. Cut around your cake board (this will be the size of your cake), cutting straight down without angling the knife inwards or outwards. For round cakes, use a small, sharp paring knife to do this and for square cakes use a large serrated one.

filling ...

Brush some sugar syrup over the cake – how much will depend on how moist you would like your cake to be. Evenly spread a layer of buttercream or ganache about 3mm (⅛in) thick over the sponge, then a thin layer of jam or conserve (jelly or preserves) if you are using any. Repeat this procedure for the next layer. Finish by adding the top layer and brushing with more sugar syrup.

coating ...

Cover the sides of the cake in buttercream or ganache, then the top – you only need a very thin and even layer. If the coating becomes 'grainy' as it picks up crumbs from the cake, put it in the refrigerator to set for about 15 minutes and go over it again with a thin second coat. Refrigerate your prepared cake for at least 1 hour so that it is firm before attempting to cover it with icing or marzipan; larger cakes will need a little longer.

sugar syrup ...

Sugar syrup is brushed on to cakes to add moisture and flavour. Ideally, this should be done while they are still warm, to help the syrup soak into the cakes. The amount of syrup used is a personal choice – if your cake is quite dry, use more syrup. However, be aware that your cake can become sweet and sticky if you use too much.

To make enough to soak a 20cm (8in) layered round cake or 12 cupcakes, put 75ml (2½fl oz) water and 75g (2¾oz) caster (superfine) sugar into a saucepan and bring to the boil, stirring once or twice. Allow to cool. Store in an airtight container in the refrigerator for up to 1 month.

preparing cupcakes ...

Before you cover the cupcakes, make sure they are completely cool. Brush with extra sugar syrup if you think they might be a bit dry or if you want them to be really moist. Not all cupcakes come out of the oven perfect – some may need some trimming with a sharp knife, while others might benefit from a little building up with an appropriate icing. Cupcakes topped with buttercream or ganache don't need to be perfectly shaped, as the icing will hide any imperfections. However, those to be covered with sugarpaste will need to be much smoother and nicely shaped.

preparing mini cakes ...

Mini cakes can be cut from larger pieces of cake or baked in special multi-mini pans. They are layered, filled and iced in a similar way to large cakes.

If cutting your own mini cakes, always choose a slightly larger size of cake than you need to allow for wastage. For nine 5cm (2in) square mini cakes, you would need an 18cm (7in) square cake.

If using multi-mini cake pans, half-fill each section of the pan with the mixture and bake. A batch of multi-mini cakes will take slightly less time to bake than a whole cake of a similar size. Leave the cakes to cool in the pans. Level the cakes by carving across the top with a large knife. Place the cakes on waxed paper, with the shaped side uppermost, and cover with a thin layer of buttercream.

baking cookies

Fundamental to any decorated cookie is the taste and shape of the cookie itself. The flavour and texture should also compliment the type of icing you plan to use. The following tips for mixing, baking and storing your cookies will ensure perfect results every time.

mixing ...

Always use the freshest ingredients for best results. Mix the dry ingredients thoroughly before mixing in the liquids. Do not over-mix the dough as this will toughen it, just mix until the flour is incorporated.

baking ...

Make sure you leave room between cookies on the baking sheet to allow them to expand a little. Try to bake cookies of a similar size in the same batch to avoid over-baking smaller cookies. Cool cookies on wire racks. This will allow the steam to evaporate and will prevent your cookies from becoming soggy.

storing ...

Most cookies have a two week shelf life, so don't be afraid to start your baking well in advance. You can even make them up to one month in advance and store them un-iced in an airtight container in the freezer.

using sugarpaste

Sugarpaste (rolled fondant) is mainly used to cover cakes, cupcakes and cookies, but it can also be cut into shapes to decorate your designs. It is available commercially in all kinds of colours. However, it is really quick and simple to colour your own paste or adjust the colour of a commercial one.

Knead the sugarpaste until it is warm and pliable. Lightly grease your work surface with white vegetable fat (shortening) or sprinkle with icing (confectioners') sugar to stop the sugarpaste from sticking. If using icing (confectioners') sugar, be aware that too much can can cause the sugarpaste to dry out and crack. Roll out the sugarpaste between spacers to ensure an even thickness.

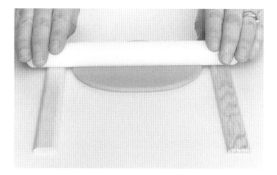

colouring sugarpaste ...

Place a little paste colour on the end of a cocktail stick, or a larger amount on a palette knife. Add the colour to the paste and knead in thoroughly, adding more until the desired effect is achieved. Be careful with pale colours, as only a little colour is needed. Deep colours, on the other hand, require plenty and will become quite sticky. To overcome this, add a pinch of gum tragacanth and leave for an hour or two.

covering cookies ...

Roll out the sugarpaste to a thickness of 3mm (⅛in) and cut out the shape of the cookie using the same cutter or template used for the cookie dough. Paint piping gel over the top of the baked cookie and place the sugarpaste onto each cookie, taking care not to stretch it out of shape.

covering cupcakes ...

Brush the cakes with sugar syrup or add a thin layer of buttercream or ganache. Roll out the sugarpaste to a thickness of 5mm (³/₁₆in). Cut out circles of sugarpaste using an appropriately sized cutter. Using a palette knife, carefully lift the paste circles onto each cupcake.

using flower paste ...

Flower paste dries quickly, so cut off only as much as you need and reseal the remainder. Work it well with your fingers – it should 'click' between your fingers when it is ready to use. If it is too hard and crumbly add a little egg white and white vegetable fat (shortening) – the fat slows down the drying process and the egg white makes it more pliable.

covering round cakes ...

1 Cut a piece of greaseproof paper or baking parchment about 7.5cm (3in) larger all round than the cake and put your cake on top.

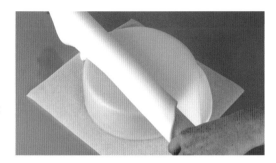

2 Roll out some sugarpaste to a thickness of about 5mm (³/₁₆in). Lift the sugarpaste with the rolling pin from the board and turn it a quarter turn before laying it down to roll again. Try to keep it a round shape so it will fit over your cake easily.

3 Pick the sugarpaste up on your rolling pin and lay it over your cake. Quickly but carefully use your hands to smooth it around and down the side of the cake. Pull the sugarpaste away from the side of the cake as you go until you reach the base, pushing out any air bubbles that may occur.

4 When the icing is on, use a smoother in a circular motion to go over the top of the cake. For the side, go around in forward circular movements, almost cutting the excess paste at the base. Trim the excess with a small, sharp knife and use the smoother to go round the cake one final time to make sure it is perfectly smooth.

covering square cakes ...

Square cakes are iced in a similar way to round cakes, but pay attention to the corners to ensure the icing doesn't tear. Use your hands to carefully cup the icing around the corners before you start working it down the sides. Mend any tears with clean soft icing as soon as possible so that the icing blends together well.

Make sure that your cake is covered with buttercream or ganache before you ice it to achieve a smooth finish

covering cake boards ...

Moisten the board with some water. Roll out the sugar paste to a thickness of 4mm (a generous ⅛in), ideally using spacers. Pick the icing up on the rolling pin and lay it over the cake board. Place the board either on a turntable or bring it towards the edge of the work surface so that the icing is hanging down over it. Use your icing smoother in a downwards motion to cut a smooth edge around the board. Cut away any excess. Finish by smoothing the top using circular movements and leave to dry overnight.

modelling with sugarpaste ...

To thicken sugarpaste for modelling, simply add CMC (Tylose) powder or gum tragacanth. As a guide, add roughly 5ml (1 tsp) of CMC (Tylose) powder or gum tragacanth to 225g (8oz) of sugarpaste and knead well. Wrap in a plastic bag and allow the gum to work before use. You will begin to feel a difference after a couple of hours, but it is best to leave it overnight. If your paste becomes crumbly or too hard to work, add a touch of white vegetable fat (shortening) and a little boiled water, and knead until softened.

When modelling characters, the different parts can be held together in various ways. Small parts can be attached with sugar glue but larger parts, such as heads and wings, will require additional support. Pieces of dry spaghetti are inserted into the models – into the hip or shoulder for example – on to which you can attach another piece – a foot, wing or head. Leave 2cm (¾in) showing at the top to support the head, and 1cm (⅜in) to support wings and feet. The pieces will still require some sugar glue to bond them, but will have more support and stay rigid. When inserting spaghetti to support heads, make sure that it is pushed into the body in a very vertical position, otherwise the head will tilt backwards and become vulnerable. The spaghetti should always be removed before eating the cake and decorations.

Sugarpaste models may also sometimes need to be supported with foam or cardboard while they are drying to prevent parts from flopping over or drooping down.

There are four basic shapes required for modelling:

❄ ball – the first step is always to roll a ball to ensure the surface is perfectly smooth, with no cracks or creases.

❄ cone – this shape is the basis for all bodies. It is made by rolling and narrowing the ball at one end, leaving it fatter at the other.

❄ sausage – arms and legs are made from this shape. It is simple to make by applying even pressure to the ball and continuing to roll, keeping the thickness uniform along the length.

❄ oval – this is used to make cheeks, ears and other small parts. It is made in the same way as the sausage, by applying even pressure to the ball, but not taking it as far.

using chocolate paste

Chocolate paste is made from Belgian chocolate, glucose and water. The glucose makes the chocolate pliable so that it can be rolled out and used to cover cakes, mould flowers and create decorations. Chocolate paste is available in white, milk and dark chocolate and various flavours, and can be used with a variety of cake decorating equipment, such as moulds and sugar shapers. It usually has a four to six month shelf life and is readily available from cake decorating shops.

chocolate paste vs. sugarpaste ...

There is a common confusion between chocolate paste and chocolate-flavoured sugarpaste. However, chocolate paste is unlike sugarpaste, as it reacts to the heat of your hands – the more you knead it, the stickier it becomes as it starts to melt. Chocolate paste must be rolled out on lots of icing (confectioners') sugar to prevent it sticking to the work surface. You may need to initially warm it for a short time (about 5–10 seconds in a microwave) if the paste is particularly hard. If you have overheated the paste and it has become extremely sticky, place it in a polythene bag, and put it in the refridgerator for an hour or until hardened.

storing chocolate paste ...

Put excess paste in a tied food-grade plastic bag and keep in cool, dry, dark conditions, away from direct sunlight and strong odours.

covering cakes with chocolate paste ...

1 Apply a thin layer of buttercream to the cake to help the chocolate paste stick.

2 Roll out the paste to a depth of about 4mm (a generous ⅛in) and lift carefully over the top of the cake, supporting it with a rolling pin, and position so that it covers the cake.

3 Smooth the surface of the cake using a smoother for the flat areas and a combination of the smoother and the palm of your hand for the curved areas.

4 Take the smoother and, while pressing down, run the flat edge around the base of the cake to create a cutting line. Trim away the excess paste with a palette knife.

Avoid working with chocolate paste in a hot environment as it melts very quickly

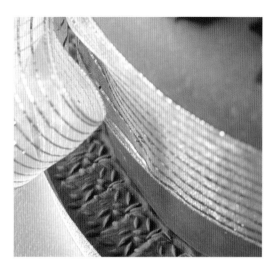

using a sugar shaper

A sugar shaper is an extremely versatile tool for use with different types of pastes. By changing the nozzle attachments, the paste can be squeezed out in various shapes to pipe lines, ribbons, tassels, sausages and more. The secret of success is to use paste of the correct consistency.

for chocolate paste ...

For best results, gently knead the chocolate paste until it is tacky before placing it into the shaper. Squeeze the shaper and use a Dresden tool to help remove the paste from it.

for sugarpaste ...

1 Knead in some gum to your sugarpaste to give it stretch. Knead in some white vegetable fat (shortening) to stop the paste getting sticky.

2 Partially dunk the paste into a small container of boiled water before kneading again (the paste should have the consistency of chewing gum).

3 Place the softened paste together with your chosen disc into the sugar shaper. Squeeze out a length of paste and remove it with a Dresden tool.

dowelling cakes

To assemble a multi-tiered cake, you need to create an internal support system to prevent it from collapsing. Dowels are designed to prevent each tier from sinking into the one underneath. They can be made from plastic or wood, but must be food graded. To dowel a cake, follow the steps below:

1 Measure the diameter of the cake you wish to place on top of the bottom tier. Cut out a piece of greaseproof paper matching the size of this smaller tier.

2 Place the greaseproof paper onto the surface of the lower cake as a guide. Gently indent the surface covered by the greaseproof paper with a dowelling rod to mark the position of each dowel. For maximum support, use at least five dowelling rods per cake plus one central rod.

3 Push one rod vertically down through the centre of the cake until it touches the cake board. Make a knife scratch or pencil mark on the dowel to mark its height in relation to the cake's surface.

4 Remove the dowel and, using a hacksaw or knife, cut on the marked line. Cut a further five rods to exactly the same size, using the cut dowel as a measure.

5 Position all six rods into the cake as marked. Spread a layer of buttercream onto the cake surface and then rest the top cake on the rods. Check the cake is level before proceeding to stack other layers on top.

using buttercream

Using buttercream is the simplest way to decorate cupcakes. To get each cake looking perfect, you will need a little practice. You can pipe the topping using a large plastic piping (pastry) bag, making a peak or swirl with either a plain or star-shaped tube (tip). Alternatively, simply use a palette knife to spread the topping on evenly to create a nice domed top.

to create a swirl ...

1 Place the piping tube (tip) in a large piping (pastry) bag, then fill half the bag with your chosen topping. Twist the top of the bag to seal.

2 Holding the bag vertically, start at the centre of the cupcake. Apply pressure to the bag and then move the tube (tip) to the edge of the cupcake and around the centre of the cake in an anti-clockwise direction.

to create a peak ...

1 Hold the bag vertically above the centre of the cupcake. Keeping the bag still, apply pressure to the bag and allow the icing to spread towards the edge of the cupcake.

2 Once it has spread as far as you wish, start to slowly lift the bag while maintaining an even pressure. When finished, release the pressure and remove the bag.

using royal icing

Royal icing is used to cover cupcakes and cookies, as well as for piping and stencilling designs. In order to pipe the icing easily, you may need to add a tiny amount of water so that the consistency is a bit softer. For stencilling, you will need a thicker consistency to ensure that the icing doesn't bleed underneath.

making a piping (pastry) bag ...

1 Cut two equal triangles from a large square piece of parchment paper. As a guide, for small bags cut from 15–20cm (6–8in) square paper and for large bags cut from 30–35cm (12–14in) square paper.

2 Keeping the centre point towards you with the longest side furthest away, curl the right-hand corner inwards and bring the point to meet the centre point. Adjust your hold so that you have the two points together between your right thumb and index finger.

3 With your left hand, curl the left point inwards, bringing it across the front and around to the back of the other two points in the centre of the cone. Adjust your grip again so that you are now holding the three points together with both your thumbs and index fingers.

4 Tighten the cone-shaped bag by gently rubbing your thumb and index fingers forwards and backwards until you have a sharp tip at the end of the bag.

5 Carefully fold the back of the bag (where all the points meet) inwards, making sure you press hard along the fold. Repeat this to make sure it is really secure.

piping with royal icing ...

1 Fill the piping (pastry) bag until it is no more than one-third full. Fold the top over, away from the join, until you have a tight and well-sealed bag. It's important to hold the bag in the correct way. Guide the bag with your index finger.

2 Touch the tube (tip) down, then lift the bag up in a smooth movement, squeezing gently. Decrease the pressure and touch it back down to the point where you want the icing to finish. Try not to drag the icing along. Use a template as a guide where possible.

3 To pipe dots, squeeze the icing out gently until you have the dot the size you require. Stop squeezing, then lift the bag. If there is a peak in the icing, use a damp brush to flatten it down.

stencilling with royal icing ...

1 Adjust the consistency of the icing if necessary. You need to have the icing fairly thick but still spreadable, so add more icing (confectioners') sugar or water as appropriate.

2 Place the stencil onto rolled out sugarpaste and carefully spread the royal icing over the stencil, removing any excess icing.

3 Once the icing is of an even thickness and you can see the outline of the pattern, gently remove the stencil taking care not to smudge the icing.

4 Immediately cut out the stencilled pattern using an appropriate circle cutter, and place it on top of a cake using a palette knife.

5 Allow the royal icing to dry (this only takes a few minutes) then, with your finger ease in any fullness in the sugarpaste. Allowing the royal icing to dry prevents it being smudged.

using cutters

There is a whole host of specialist sugarcraft cutters available in various shapes, sizes and designs. They are very simple to use and the results can be quite dramatic! There are two techniques for using cutters:

cutting simple shapes ...

1 Press down onto your paste with the cutter, wiggle the cutter fractionally from side to side to give a cleaner cut.

2 Remove the excess paste, and ideally leave your paste on your work board for a minute or two before lifting it with a palette knife.

cutting intricate shapes ...

1 To get a clean cut, rather than pressing a cutter into the paste, place the paste over the cutter and roll over with a rolling pin.

2 Run your finger over the edges of the cutter, then turn the cutter over and carefully press out the paste using a soft paintbrush.

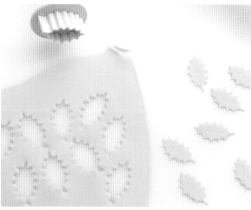

cookie cutters ...

Whether you want a classic gingerbread man or luscious lips, you will be spoilt for choice by the range of cutters available. For cheap and cheerful cutters that do the job, choose from an array of mass-produced, colourful plastic cutters. Tinplate cutters are also low cost but have to be cared for as they are prone to rust. Handcrafted copper and stainless steel cutters are more of an investment but they are strong, safe and hold their shape after years of repeated use. Stainless steel cutters are even dishwasher friendly!

templates ...

If you can't find a suitable cutter, one option to consider is making and using a template instead. Find an image that appeals to you and resize it using a computer or photocopier. Trace the image onto tracing paper and transfer it onto card. Cut around the traced outline of the card to produce your template. This is very easy to do for basic shapes, such as circles and squares, if you don't have the right cutter.

using chocolate

Chocolate contains cocoa butter crystals and tempering is a process of heating chocolate so that these crystals are uniform. Correctly tempered chocolate will produce an end result that is smooth-tasting, crisp, even-coloured and shiny, while incorrectly tempered chocolate produces a dull or streaky end result often referred to as a 'bloom', which while not inedible, does look unsightly and will taste grainy. Incorrectly tempered chocolate will not set very well, will 'bend' rather than 'snap', and will not release easily from moulds, so before placing chocolate into a mould ensure it is correctly tempered.

types of chocolate ...

There are two types of chocolate available: couverture chocolate and confectioner's coating chocolate, but all of the items in this book require couverture chocolate which usually contains a minimum of 32 per cent cocoa butter and tastes far superior to coating chocolate, which can contain little or no cocoa butter. Couverture chocolate must go through the process of tempering prior to use in order to produce a shiny chocolate that 'snaps' when broken. If you are mixing chocolate together with other ingredients, it will not need to be tempered.

tempering chocolate ...

The simplest method is to purchase chocolate couverture callets or buttons, which have already been through one of the processes of tempering. With extreme care, these can be melted in a small plastic bowl in the microwave in short 10-second bursts on full power (850w), mixing thoroughly between each interval. Alternatively, follow the steps below:

1 Melt the chocolate to 45°C (113°F) over a double boiler, being extremely careful not to allow any steam or water to come into contact with the chocolate. Once the chocolate is melted, remove from the heat.

2 Add approximately one-third again of couverture callets to the melted chocolate and stir until melted. This will begin to bring the temperature of the chocolate down. Using a chocolate thermometer, dark chocolate should be cooled to 31°C (88°F), milk chocolate to 30°C (86°F), and white chocolate to 29°C (84°F).

3 Dip a clean palette knife into the chocolate to test it. Allow it to set for 2–3minutes. If it sets hard, snaps easily and has a shiny gloss, it is ready for use.

Tempered chocolate is useful for attaching edible embellishments to your creations

using moulds with chocolate paste ...

Silicone rubber moulds can be used with chocolate paste to make a variety of shapes. When working with chocolate paste, it is easier to use shallow moulds with clear, defined detail, as otherwise it can be difficult to remove the paste.

1 Briefly knead a piece of chocolate paste with a little icing (confectioners') sugar.

2 Press the paste into the mould and gently bend the mould back to release the shape. The paste shape can be attached to your creation using a little tempered chocolate.

using moulds with tempered chocolate ...

When working with tempered chocolate, use plastic moulds as they provide a firmer foundation.

1 Temper your chocolate. Warm the mould gently using a dry heat. Place the tempered chocolate in a disposable piping (pastry) bag and pipe into the mould.

2 Tap the mould gently to allow any air bubbles to come to the surface. Place the mould in the fridge to completely set for 20 minutes.

3 Carefully tip the mould to release the chocolate.

using transfer sheets ...

Transfer sheets are acetate sheets with an edible pattern embossed onto them with cocoa butter. When covered with tempered chocolate, the heat reacts with the cocoa butter to transfer the pattern onto the chocolate. Available in a variety of colours and designs, transfer sheets can be used to decorate chocolate shards, make cut out shapes or wrap around cakes for dramatic effect.

1 Lay a transfer sheet onto your work surface with the embossed cocoa butter print facing upwards.

2 Temper some chocolate and pour it onto the sheet. Use a palette knife to spread the chocolate in an even, thin layer across the transfer sheet.

3 Allow the chocolate to dry completely then carefully remove the transfer sheet to leave the pattern imprinted onto the chocolate.

4 If you are making shards or shapes, wait for about 2–3 minutes for the chocolate to start to 'dull' then cut out your shapes. Leave to dry completely before removing the acetate sheet.

transfer sheet tips ...

❊ Think carefully about which chocolate to use with your transfer sheet. Snowflake designs, for example, would be lost using white chocolate.

❊ Transfer sheets have a single use only. Once the pattern has been printed it will become a plain sheet of acetate.

❊ Transfer sheets should be stored in a cool dry place, away from sunlight to prevent any colour fade.

suppliers

UK

Lindy's Cakes Ltd
Unit 2, Station Approach,
Wendover, Aylesbury,
Buckinghamshire, HP22 6BN
Tel: 01296 622418
www.lindyscakes.co.uk

Tracey's Cakes Ltd
5 Wheelwright Road, Longwick,
Buckinghamshire, HP27 9ST
Tel: 01844 347147
www.traceyscakes.co.uk

Maisie's World
840 High Lane, Chell, Stoke on
Trent, Staffordshire, ST6 6HG
Tel: 01782 876090
www.maisieparrish.com

The Cake Parlour
146 Arthur Road, London,
SW19 8AQ
Tel: 020 8947 4424
www.thecakeparlour.com

Home Chocolate Factory
Unit 1750, SafeStore,
1,000 North Circular Road,
London , NW2 7JP
Tel: 020 8450 1523
www.homechocolatefactory.com

A Piece of Cake
18–20 Upper High Street,
Thame, Oxon , OX9 3EX
Tel: 01844 213428
www.sugaricing.com

Blue Ribbons
29 Walton Road, East Molesey,
Surrey, KT8 0DH
Tel: 020 8941 1591
www.blueribbons.co.uk

Squire's Kitchen
3 Waverley Lane,
Farnham, Surrey,
GU9 8BB
Tel: 0845 6171 810
www.squires-shop.com

FMM Sugarcraft
Unit 7, Chancerygate Business
Park, Whiteleaf Road, Hemel
Hempstead, Herts, HP3 9HD
Tel: 01442 292970
www.fmmsugarcraft.com

Sugarshack
Unit 12, Bowmans Trading
Estate, Westmoreland Road,
London, NW9 9RL
Tel: 020 8204 2994
www.sugarshack.co.uk

Knightbridge PME Ltd
Chadwell Heath Lane,
Romford, Essex, RN6 4NP
Tel: 020 8590 5959
www.cakedecoration.co.uk

Orchard Products
51 Hallyburton Road, Hove,
East Sussex, BN3 7GP
Tel: 01273 419418
www.orchardproducts.co.uk

US

First Impressions Molds

300 Business Park Way,
Suite A-200, Royal Palm
Beach, FL 33411
Tel: 561 784 7186
www.firstimpressionsmolds.com

New York Cake Supplies

56 West 22nd Street,
New York, NY 10010
Tel: 800 942 2539
www.nycake.com

Wilton Industries Inc.

2240 West 75th Street,
Woodridge, IL 60517
Tel: 800 794 5866
www.wilton.com

Chocolate Man

16580 35th Ave NE,
Lake Forest Park,
WA 98155-6606
Tel: 206 365 2025
www.chocolateman.com

Global Sugar Art

625 Route 3, Unit 3,
Plattsburgh,NY 12901
Tel: 518 561 3039
www.globalsugarart.com

All In One Bake Shop

8566 Research Boulevard,
Austin, TX 78758
Tel: 512 371 3401
www.allinonebakeshop.com

Country Kitchen Sweet Art

4621 Speedway Drive Fort,
Wayne, IN 46825
Tel: 800 497 3927
www.countrykitchensa.com

Copper Gifts

900 North 32nd Street,
Parsons, KS 67357
Tel: 620 421 0654
www.coppergifts.com

US cup measurements

If you prefer to use cup measurements, please use the following
conversions. (Note: 1 Australian tbsp = 20ml)

liquid

1 tsp = 5ml
1 tbsp = 15ml
½ cup = 125ml/4fl oz
1 cup = 225ml/8fl oz

butter

1 tbsp = 15g/1/2oz
2 tbsp = 25g//1oz
½ cup/1 stick = 115g/4oz
1 cup/2 sticks = 225g/8oz

caster (superfine) sugar/brown sugar

½ cup = 100g/3½oz
1 cup = 200g/7oz

icing (confectioners') sugar

1 cup = 115g/4oz

flour

1 cup = 140g/5oz

double (heavy) cream

1 cup = 225g/8oz

author credits

The publishers would like to thank the following authors who have allowed the reproduction of their designs in this book.

Lindy Smith for Fabulous Firs, Winter Frost, Gingerbread Scene, Beautiful Baubles, Snowy Stockings, Cookie Crackers, Festive Fancies and Heavenly Angel

Tracey Mann for Chocolate Wreath, Brilliant Brownies, Snowflake Sensation, Treasure Trove, Chocolate Drops, Star of Wonder and Tempting Truffles

Zoe Clark for All Wrapped Up, Marzipan Trees and Candy Cane Treats

Maisie Parrish for Winter Wonderland and Pretty Parcels

Joan & Graham Belgrove for We Three Kings and Mistletoe Magic

index

loved this book?

Tell us what you think and you could win another fantastic book from David & Charles in our monthly prize draw.

www.lovethisbook.co.uk

Bake Me I'm Yours...
Whoopie Pies

Natalie Saville & Jill Collins

ISBN-13: 978-1-4463-0068-8

Over 70 great excuses to bake, fill and decorate these tempting treats! Includes everything you need to create stunning whoopie pies for your special occasions.

Bake Me I'm Yours...
Cupcake Love

Zoe Clark

ISBN-13: 978-0-7153-3781-3

An indulgent collection of cupcake projects, recipes and ideas for every romantic occasion. Tempt loved ones with the 20 gorgeous designs.

Celebrate with Mini Cakes

Lindy Smith

ISBN-13: 978-0-7153-3783-7

Features designs and techniques for over 20 celebration mini cakes. Create delicious treats for every occasion, from birthdays and children's parties to weddings and Christmas.

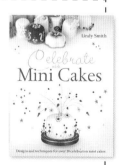

Fun & Original Birthday Cakes

Maisie Parrish

ISBN-13: 978-0-7153-3833-9

Be amused and amazed by this incredible collection of brilliant birthday cakes. Add a personal touch to your celebrations with over 30 unique characters, decorations and toppers to delight loved ones.